Your $7500 *Dream Wedding!*

How to Plan Your Dream Wedding For $7500

D.A. LAING

Copyright, Legal Notice and Disclaimer

This publication is protected under the *Canadian Copyright Act* and all other applicable international, federal, provincial/state and local laws. All rights are reserved, including resale rights: you are not allowed to give or sell this guide to anyone else.

Please note that much of this publication is based on personal experience and anecdotal evidence. Although the author has made every reasonable attempt to achieve complete accuracy of the content in this guide, they assume no responsibility for errors or omissions. Also, you should use this information as you see fit, and at your own risk. Your particular situation may not be exactly suited to the examples illustrated here; in fact, it's likely that they won't be the same, and you should adjust your use of the information and recommendations accordingly.

Any trademarks, service marks, product names or named features are assumed to be the property of their respective owners and are used only for reference. There is no implied endorsement if we use one of these terms.

Finally, use your head. Nothing in this guide is intended to replace common sense or legal, medical or other professional advice; it is meant to inform and entertain the reader. So have fun with *Your* $7500 *Dream Wedding*.

TABLE OF CONTENTS

❧ Introduction ❧

The average North American wedding costs between $20,000 and $30,000. At the time of our wedding, my wife, Tory, was 26 and I was 27. I had just bought a house and Tory had just completed two university degrees. Needless to say, we were on a very tight budget and could not afford such a costly wedding.

Tory and I viewed our wedding as a celebration to kick off our life together; however, we did not want to go into much (if any) debt, if it all possible. I suggested to Tory that we could have a big blowout bash on our 10th or 15th anniversary, when we'd likely be in a better financial situation, but that I didn't want to start our married life in any more debt than we already were.

We tossed around the idea of a destination wedding, inviting only our closest friends and immediate family to join us at a resort in the Caribbean. The resorts take care of everything, from catering to decorating to photos, and you're already at your honeymoon spot. The trouble is that this type of wedding would have put a lot of financial pressure on our guests, and we wouldn't have been able to have nearly as many people attend; maybe only a handful. The main reason we decided to have a more traditional wedding locally was so that all the people we wanted to help us celebrate would be able to attend.

With some careful planning, and a lot of help from family and friends, our wedding day was beautiful, and we will treasure the celebration for the rest of our lives. Often people come up to Tory and I to tell us that ours was the best wedding they'd ever attended. Some even tell us that they want their wedding to be just like ours.

On that basis this book was conceived. It is intended as a guide, not a manual. You may spend more and you may spend less on your wedding, and where you spend your money will depend on what's important to you.

I've prepared a sample budget (presented at the end of the book) to give you an idea of where your money will go as you prepare for your wedding. The figures in this budget are only targets for frugal wedding planners and all of the items were available at the prices I've quoted at the time of writing; however, not necessarily in all areas. To plan your perfect frugal wedding, creativity and flexibility are required. Most important: enjoy!

❧ PLANNING ❧

"Marriage: a book of which the first chapter is written in poetry and the remaining chapters written in prose."

— BEVERLY NICHOLS

CHAPTER 1: THE PEOPLE

Remember that a wedding is a celebration of your new life together. This day is for you and your new spouse to celebrate your commitment to each other with your family and friends. There are people who take their wedding as an opportunity to impress their friends, family and business acquaintances by planning for what they think their guests will want. That's their prerogative, and if you want to do that, then go ahead and have fun. However, if you've purchased this book, then you're likely part of the other 90% of the population and are interested in making your day wonderful **and** affordable.

Your $7500 *Dream Wedding!*

To make your day affordable and memorable, plan to spend money on the things that will make your day more personal and perhaps skip or substitute the traditions that are associated with weddings that are really more for show. Bottom line, what is going to make the celebration fun and memorable, not a show.

GUEST LIST

Think about this: a wedding is a celebration that you want to share with those that mean the most to you. Why is it then that some people invite family members they've never met and business acquaintances of their parents? The more people at your wedding, the bigger the bill, so keep it simple and keep it small. Remember this when developing your guest list. Some people have huge families with 50 or more cousins and 25 uncles and aunts and lots of friends. If this is your situation, then you'll have to really think about who is actually close to you and who you want to share this day with. Are you inviting people you met once at a family reunion 10 years ago? Other young couples find themselves being pressured by parents to invite business associates and such. This is your day, so ask yourself an important question: "Am I inviting this person because I truly want them to share my wedding day with me, or would I be inviting them simply as a courtesy?"

What's an affordable number of guests? For a frugal wedding, a reasonable number of people would be roughly 100. That was the size of our wedding and it was quite manageable. Also, as I will demonstrate throughout this book (particularly in the reception section), it is an affordable number. If you can reduce the number of guests, then you can spend even less money.

Developing the guest list is very challenging, but once you have chosen a maximum number, stick to it. One way to limit numbers is to limit guests of guests. You may have some people on your list that don't know your family and aren't associated with any of your other friends. They should be invited to bring a guest so that they can fully enjoy your celebration and you don't have to worry about whether they are having a good time. In many cases, however, your guests will come in pairs anyway. Also, the people in your groups of friends will mostly attend, and they will have a blast hanging out together. Those in these groups that do not have significant others that are known to the group may be happier not having to entertain a guest.

Of course, when you are sending out the invitations, you don't want to be rude and flatly state, "Don't bring a guest." Perhaps a note something like the following could be included in the appropriate invitations:

Because we want all of our nearest friends and family to celebrate this special day with us, and because of space constraints at our reception venue, unfortunately we are unable to accommodate a guest.

You should also follow this up with an e-mail or phone call and explain honestly that your budget is restricted and you are trying to stick to throwing a great wedding without blowing the bank. I guarantee you they'll understand, and none of your friends or family will give you grief over this. Remember, you want all of your guests to be at ease and having fun celebrating with you. That's the whole point!

WEDDING PARTY

The wedding party consists of the bridesmaids and groomsmen, and normally the bride will have a maid of honor and the groom will have a best man. Think of who in your life is closest to you and choose them to be in your wedding party. It's great to be able to involve your best friends in your wedding day. One financial consideration is that the larger the wedding party, potentially the larger your transportation costs.

INVITATIONS

Attractive invitations for your wedding can be a nice memento of your special day and adds to the overall excitement and special feeling. Though invitations can be expensive, they don't have to be. Having invitations designed and printed can cost anywhere from $150 to over $500. Typically, when you receive an invitation to a wedding, it will contain several items aside from the invitation itself. When you open the envelope you will normally see the invitation on a high-quality card stock, a small RSVP card containing certain information (such as meal choice and the number of attendees) and a postage paid envelope for the RSVP card. Sometimes there will also be a small map with directions to your venue(s).

These days, you will find that most people find it a bit of a hassle to RSVP via snail mail. Instead, have people RSVP by e-mail or telephone. You will likely find that people respond much more quickly since most are on the Internet almost every day. It also saves them a trip down to the mailbox, and it can save you nearly $100. You can find really good quality invitations without the RSVP card and RSVP envelope for roughly $150 to $200.

CHAPTER 2: THE CLOTHES

WEDDING DRESS

The reality of it is that not every blushing bride can afford the latest from Vera Wang. That doesn't mean you won't be the star of the show, the talk of the town or the belle of the ball. When purchasing a wedding dress, it's important to keep things in perspective. Your wedding ring will last forever, but your wedding dress will likely only be worn for eight hours or less.

Buying a wedding dress can be very emotional. For some, finding the perfect dress is related to their childhood dream of an ideal wedding;

others are loathe to start the process. Regardless of how you feel about buying a wedding dress, rest assured that there are plenty of options to suit every bride's needs.

Buying a wedding dress doesn't have to be about sacrifice; really it's about being savvy. There are plenty of great ways to get the dress of your dreams without breaking the bank. This chapter provides a number of suggestions of where you can find the dress of your dreams and how you can save money while you're at it.

BRIDAL SHOPS

Some women can't wait to find themselves amidst the thousands of dresses at their local bridal shop; others are overwhelmed by the thought of so many dresses and so many different styles. If you do decide to stake out the selection at a bridal store, here are some tips which may save you hundreds of dollars.

- Almost all bridal stores have a section where you can buy samples or floor models off the rack, and these are often priced at a substantial discount.

- Most bridal shops have sales after June. So, if you have time, be sure to continually check the sale section for new additions.

- If you are unable to find a dress off the rack, take the time to comparison shop. Take down the name of the designer and the style of the dress. You may be surprised at the price differences between one bridal shop and the next.

ALTERNATIVES TO BRIDAL SHOPS

If shopping a bridal boutique is not for you, don't worry, there are a number of other avenues available to you, some of which won't even require you to leave the comfort of your home.

Your $7500 Dream Wedding!

The Internet provides a number of fantastic resources right at your fingertips.

- ✂ Lightinthebox.com allows you to search for dresses of all different styles and order one wholesale, saving you hundreds of dollars. This is a fantastic resource that definitely can't be overlooked. The best part of it is, they will ship to anywhere in the world. This resource will allow you to find a beautiful dress and only have to spend a couple of hundred dollars.

- ✂ You can also try searching for wedding dresses on eBay. Some of the dresses are barely used and others have never been used at all. Often these dresses will be sold at highly reduced prices.

- ✂ Another excellent way to find well priced wedding dresses online is by browsing wedding-related message boards for women looking to sell their dresses or accessories.

An alternative to online shopping is your local consignment or second hand shop. If they happen to have something you love, the price will likely be much less than you could get at a bridal shop. Also, if you or someone you know is talented with a sewing machine you may be able to customize the dress to suit your own needs.

Depending on the type of wedding you are planning, you may even be able to find your wedding dress in the evening wear section of your local department store. It never hurts to check out the selection, and you may just save yourself some money.

In some cities there are stores that rent wedding dresses. If your city has such a store, you may be able to save yourself hundreds of dollars by renting instead of buying.

Before you prepare yourself to drop hundreds of dollars on the wedding dress of your dreams, you may want to ask your mother or your grandmother about the dress they wore on their wedding day. Wearing the dress worn by your mother or grandmother will not only save you a ton of money, it will also be sentimental for you and your family.

Regardless of where you end up looking for your perfect gown, remember to be patient, savvy and smart; it'll end up saving you money.

BRIDAL ACCESSORIES

You can choose from any number of bridal accessories for your big day. Accessories can be costly, and if you're trying to stick to a budget, this is a great area for you to save some cash. One sure fire way to save money is by being smart about where you get your accessories. Borrowing jewelry from your mom or grandmother is not only meaningful, it's also a great way to save money. Also, talk to your friends and family to see if you can borrow the veil or tiara that they wore on their wedding day. If you're having trouble finding accessories to borrow, you may be able to find what you're looking for at a consignment or second hand shop.

Another way to save money is by making your own veil. If you're talented at sewing or just looking for a challenge, finding a pattern for a veil, buying tulle at a fabric store and sewing it yourself can save you a couple of hundred dollars.

If your dress is floor length, consider wearing shoes that you already own. No one is going to be able to see what you're wearing on your feet and this will give you an extra $50 to $100 to spend somewhere else in your budget. (And you can probably get away with something way more comfortable, which will allow you to enjoy your celebration that much more. I know of a woman who wore white running shoes with shimmery satin bows for laces under her full-length wedding gown—she danced all night!)

BRIDESMAIDS

If you are sticking to a tight budget, one way to help stay on track is to ask your bridal party to purchase their own dresses. Most women who are asked to be in a wedding party expect to buy their own dresses.

GROOM AND GROOMSMEN

Having the groomsmen pay for their own tuxedo rental is common, and it will keep your costs down. The best way to find a rental tux is to go into a high-end menswear store or a formal wear store and they will work with you to help you find what it is that you like. These stores usually have up-to-date styles and you can rent everything from hats to shoes and anything in between. A number of stores offer a deal that allows the groom to receive his tux free of charge when a certain number of tuxedos are ordered for the groomsmen.

Each of the groomsmen will have to go into the store to get fitted, and the week prior to the wedding, the tuxedos will be ready. The groom and groomsmen will have to go in once again and to make sure that the outfits fit. Higher end companies are usually pretty accurate off the bat and everything should fit pretty well. If something doesn't quite fit properly, they can send it out and have it back in the proper fit within 24 to 48 hours. If any of the groomsmen live out of town, they can go to a menswear shop in their area to get measured and call their measurements into the store that is handling the rentals.

Shop around to find a good deal and to ask about getting a free tux for the groom. When you go into a store to organize tuxedos for your side of the wedding party, you will likely be expected to pay a deposit to process the rental order. If the groom is receiving his tux for free, usually it's courtesy that he pays the deposit for the groomsmen, which is normally only about $20 per outfit.

◈ CEREMONY ◈

"There is no more lovely, friendly and charming relationship, communion or company than a good marriage."

◯— MARTIN LUTHER

CHAPTER 3: THE LOCATION

By far, the most inexpensive way to have a wedding is to get married on a family or friends' property. If you know someone that has a beautiful property that's large enough for a ceremony and reception, it can be an excellent way to save money.

Many people choose to be married in a church. This is normally only a few hundred dollars for the minister/priest and for the church itself. If you're a member of a church, often the church rental is free.

When decorating the ceremony venue, keep it very simple. Perhaps flowers placed near the altar or on the sides of pews. Some candles on a table near the altar or behind the minister is very elegant as well.

Being married outdoors is also popular and inexpensive; however, there should be a backup plan in case of rain. Having a nice arch or trellis adds to the overall beauty, but the great thing about outdoor weddings is that the natural beauty of the surroundings is often enough. If you plan to have your wedding in a public place, such as a park, lakeside area or beach, you may need to get permission from the local municipality.

As part of the ceremony, you can have a friend or family member read a passage of scripture or a poem that is meaningful. As people are filing into the church, you could have a CD playing some gentle music or you could elect to have a pianist perhaps play some music while your guests are arriving and taking their seats.

Of course, the cheapest way to get married (though it's not typically all that popular with younger couples) is to have a civil marriage ceremony conducted at your local city hall or town hall. Usually there is a set date and time, such as every Friday at 1:30 pm, when you can meet with the officiant and, for a fee of around $200, you can be married. Some people just want a simple ceremony and to have a couple of family members and maybe one friend each.

CHAPTER 4: THE PICTURES

A great way to remember your wedding day is by hiring a professional photographer. If you are friends with one or have one in your family, then you've lucked out. Like many wedding-oriented services, photographers vary in price and it definitely helps to shop around. You should be able to find a three-to-five-hour package for under $1000. This should be enough time for the photographer to take pictures during the ceremony, afterwards outside the church and at whatever other location you may choose. You can also have the photographer present during the reception; however, this may cost a little more. Get quotes from a number of photographers, asking what sort of package is available without going over $1000.

Normally a wedding package will include several hundred images that will be provided either on disks or posted on a private gallery online through the photographer's website. You order prints either online or with the photographer directly. A certain number of prints will be included in the original package, and you will be able to order more at an extra charge.

When you're interviewing photographers, ask to see an entire wedding rather than just a few shots from multiple weddings. This way you will be able to see the general quality of their work rather than just the best pieces.

Before the wedding day, take a look at where you want your pictures to be taken. Inform your photographer about your location so that they can make themselves familiar with it. A local photographer should also have ideas about some nice places to take wedding photos. Having an area in mind is helpful because it saves time, and the photographer can tell everyone where to stand and how to get in place. The sooner you get your pictures done, the sooner you can get to the reception. Also it can be very costly to have the photographer stay for longer than the originally contracted time, so having an idea about where your pictures will be taken is important.

You may also want to think about where you'll have your pictures taken in the event that it rains. There may be some nice old halls or galleries or museums in your area where you could have your pictures taken after the ceremony.

VIDEOGRAPHY

Videographers can produce high-quality and professional videos as keepsakes of your wedding day; however, they tend to be expensive. You will find that videography packages cost thousands of dollars, so I wouldn't recommend it. You'll find that you will get a lot more use out of pictures because you can enlarge them and display them so that you can enjoy them every single day. Digital cameras with video capture are so commonplace these days that you can have a friend or family member capture your wedding ceremony on video, though it won't be as high quality. Having a proper photographer is more important and, in my opinion, that's where you should spend your money.

CHAPTER 5: THE TRANSPORTATION

Though it's not necessary, it's great if you can provide transportation for yourself, the wedding party and your family from your wedding venue to the area where pictures are going to be taken and then to the reception hall. Of course, if you are getting married on someone's property, all of this would happen at the same location and you will save a lot of money.

You can handle transportation several ways. One way is to have everyone drive themselves, with the bride and groom riding in the same vehicle as the best man and maid of honor. If you know anyone that has a really nice car, perhaps you can use that rather than riding in the back of your rusted out '86 Cutlass. Otherwise, you're going to need something with style. Depending on the size of your wedding party, this could add up to a big expense.

A great option that is cheaper than going with a limo and will definitely add high style to your wedding day is to rent an exotic or luxury vehicle. You may not be able to fit your entire wedding party in it, but you could perhaps take the best man and maid of honor with you. If you rent a Hummer or other big luxury SUV, you could fit some family in there as well. A large luxury vehicle can cost as little as $300 to $400 for the entire day, you just have to do without the chauffeur.

You may also decide that you want a little alone time and that you and your new spouse will take one car while the others follow. You could rent a nice sports car, like a Porsche or Corvette or even a Dodge Viper, for a few hundred dollars a day. Or, if it's more your style, you could rent a nice big BMW or Mercedes Benz. Not only will it give your wedding day that special feeling, it will also make you look great in your wedding pictures!

If you've got your heart set on a big, stretch limousine, the most economical way is to just hire one 10 passenger limo for a few hours. This way you can have the bride transported to the ceremony location, then the bride and groom along with the best man, maid of honor and parents can ride in the limousine together. Everyone else will be able to follow along in their own vehicles. Doing it this way will still ensure that your day is special but should allow you to keep your transportation costs under $700.

❧ RECEPTION ❧

"We are told that people stay in love because of chemistry, or because they remain intrigued with each other, because of many kindnesses, because of luck. But part of it has got to be forgiveness and gratefulness."

— ELLEN GOODMAN

The wedding reception is the big ticket event in any wedding. It's where the bulk of the costs stem from, and it's normally what guests remember. This is where a lot of young couples put themselves into debt for years, planning a massive bash that costs them tens of thousands of dollars. You can have a great, elegant evening without paying for it for years to come.

CHAPTER 6: THE VENUE

Where you plan to hold your reception will determine if you can meet your $7500 budget or not. A lot of couples find it easier to just let someone else take care of all the details for them. That's the expensive way to do it. I'm going to show you how to do it easily, and cheaply. Forget wedding halls and banquet halls that do all of the decorating and catering for you. You need to find a place that you can decorate, cater and serve your own liquor in. This is **definitely** a must! Look around at banquet halls and golf clubs that do not permit outside catering and liquor, and you will see that your catering and bar costs will soar!

If you are lucky enough to know someone with a beautiful house and property, and you plan to have the ceremony and reception there, then consider having a fall back in case it rains. Booking a hall just in case is a good option.

Local halls can be a very inexpensive place to hold your reception. Many universities have reception and banquet halls that can be rented at low cost, and they're usually quite elegant. The main point is that you need to be able to provide your own catering and bar service. This is where you'll really save your money.

Perhaps you know someone that is in the military. Tory and I had our wedding at a local officers' mess. It was very elegant and very inexpensive. We used military stewards to work behind the bar, and though we also had to pay for a duty officer to be present during the reception, all of the staff were a great help and did a wonderful job. The mess and the staff were only a few hundred dollars. We saved money by decorating the mess ourselves and providing our own catering. Tables, chairs and drink glasses were all included with the rental of the mess, and the caterer that we used was familiar with the building.

You may not know someone in the military, but perhaps you know someone that is a member of a legion or veterans' association. Perhaps a local museum or building in a national historic trust would work for you. Some of them have beautiful gardens and grand rooms that can be rented at fairly low cost. With these sorts of rentals, however, you should make it clear with the building management the type of reception that you have in mind to ensure that it is appropriate and allowed.

Country cottages have a lot of charm and can provide beautiful views. If you have a smaller wedding, you may find that a small country cottage may be the perfect thing for you. You may find a beautiful luxury cottage on a lake or in the country that may only cost you a couple of hundred dollars per night, which would give you access the day before to decorate and allow the caterer to set up if necessary. This may also provide excellent opportunities for your photographer to shoot with a lake or rolling countryside as a backdrop.

Get married on a weekday. Have you ever considered getting married on a Friday for example? This can save you a lot of money on a venue because typically weekends are more expensive.

Chapter 7: The Decorations

The best way to keep your budget within $7500 is to rent a hall or use a venue where you can do everything yourself. Decorating is one of the things you can save a lot of money on and it doesn't have to be difficult. The main point is to keep it simple and pick out a few key items that will make your reception look very elegant and classy.

The most obvious place to start when thinking about decorating your reception area is the dinner tables. When looking for a caterer, try to find one that supplies all of the linens. This will make your job much easier because they will bring good-quality tablecloths and napkins. When checking out the hall, take measurements of all tables that will require a tablecloth because the caterer will need to know what size linens you will need.

Depending on the layout of your venue, you may find it helpful to have some pub-style tables available for people to stand around. At our wedding, we didn't have the floor space to put enough tables to accommodate everyone: we only had dinner tables to seat 64 people and we had 100 attending. The caterer suggested we put some pub tables around the dance floor, where four people could stand around and eat. These tables would also be useful once dinner was over and people were drinking and milling about. If you have the space to fit enough dinner tables for everyone, you may still consider having a couple of pub tables because they are great for the party part of the reception. Unlike the dinner tables, these tables weren't provided by the venue, so we had to rent them; however, they were inexpensive at around $8 each. We had four of these tables, so we could accommodate another 16 for dinner, and the remaining 20 people sat on sofas and comfortable chairs that were a part of the officers' mess. Eating on your lap is normally not a comfortable or easy task, so the caterer created a dinner that included only food that could be eaten using a fork (such as chicken satays with a spicy peanut sauce, various seafood items and meats that were pre-cut). You may be thinking that this doesn't sound like the elegant dinner you had in mind, but I can tell you that people absolutely loved it. Because the style of dining was more relaxed, everyone felt comfortable to mingle and walk around and really enjoy the party atmosphere. The hall was decorated elegantly, so it didn't feel cheap, and the food was outstanding.

Another decorating consideration is the center pieces for the tables. Once again, by doing this yourself you can save hundreds of dollars. For our wedding, my wife bought some tall clear glass vases from a dollar store and made a simple seasonal bouquet. Rather than buying expensive flowers for your centerpieces, figure out what flowers and grasses are in season and then experiment until you find an arrangement that suits your theme. If flowers are important for you and want to have a florist make your centerpieces, one way to save money is to have the florist use flowers that are in season—out-of-season flowers are much more expensive. For the pub tables, we bought some simple martini glasses from a dollar store, added some water beads and placed a flower into the glass—the effect was beautiful. For a couple of dollars each, we had a creative centerpiece that our guests found intriguing.

Now you've got the dinner tables and pub tables decorated, you'll want to add a few more decorative items around the room to give it a more festive, elegant feel. One way to do this is to perhaps put up a few fake trees then string some white lights around them. The fake trees can be expensive if bought new, but check out second hand and thrift shops where you can often purchase trees or other fake plants for only a few dollars. Also, many people have beautiful silk trees or large plants in their homes, so it's worth seeing if you can borrow from a friend or relative.

Another decorating requirement for the dining area is chair covers. You will find that the chairs at most halls are of the cheap stackable variety, so chair covers are a necessity. It's relatively inexpensive to rent chair covers, and they make a world of difference in transforming your venue into the elegant event that it deserves to be. Your caterer may rent chair covers (maybe for as little as $1.50 per chair), but they can also be rented from most wedding and event rental businesses. You can also find them available for rent online, where they can be as cheap as $1.75 per cover. For 100 chairs, that's only $150 to $175 plus tax, for a truly necessary decorating item.

Chapter 8: The Food and Drink

Keeping It Fun and Elegant

If you want to have a fun, inexpensive wedding, consider departing from the traditional. Rather than having a formal sit down dinner, with endless courses being served and fancy desserts, think about going buffet style, which can be significantly less costly. It also gives people the opportunity to socialize more and can make your event have a lighter, more fun, party atmosphere. Rather than assigned seating, allowing people to sit wherever they want promotes socializing, so people aren't sitting at one table all night talking to all the same people.

Planning the reception dinner this way will save you money because you don't need place cards, you don't need people to RSVP their dinner order and you don't have to worry about seating divorcées at tables away from their exes...they'll do it on their own. You also pay for far fewer servers using a buffet-style meal.

Catering

Though catering can be one of the biggest expenses of your wedding reception, it doesn't have to be. Finding a venue that will allow you to cater your own food will help a lot because it gives you the freedom to shop around and find the best deal. Also, as discussed earlier, by restricting your guest list to no more than 100 people, you will cut down your catering bill significantly. Though there are many excellent caterers that are also very reasonably priced, another option is local colleges and universities that offer hospitality services programs that provide budget-conscious catering.

Whether you choose a professional caterer or seek out hospitality programs, you should be able to cater a really nice dinner, whether it's sit down or buffet style, for about $20 per plate, which would bring your bill to around $2000. When checking out different caterers, make sure that you ask if they provide linens, plates, cutlery and glasses, or whether that is an extra charge. Keep in mind that you will have to pay for servers and taxes as well, which will be an extra couple of hundred dollars. All in, you should aim for a catering budget of about $2500.

Normally, when you meet with a caterer, they will have a few standard menus that you can choose from, but all of these menus can be adjusted. As you are planning your meal, you should bear in mind not only general food preferences, but also whether or not there will be any guests with food allergies or specific food limitations, such as vegetarians, and the layout and seating arrangements at your venue.

Ideally, you want to find a local caterer that knows the specific hall you're going to use; however, that's not absolutely necessary. If you're using a caterer that's unfamiliar with your venue, you'll need to find out information about kitchen facilities to provide to the caterer. You will need to know what there is in the way of refrigerators, freezers, ovens, stoves, dishwashers, sinks and prep areas. Some halls will have a limited kitchen with only a fridge and a prep area where the caterer can set all the prepared food and put it together to serve. Other halls will have complete kitchens with full cooking facilities.

Cake

The legendary status of the wedding cake can lead some couples to spend thousands of dollars for this one element of the entire celebration. Of course it would be incredible to look at and yes the message it sends is that you've spent a lot of money. But, will people really be impressed? I doubt anyone is even likely to remember.

It is your wedding day and, being a special day, there should probably be some sort of cake. One of Tory's friends happens to be exceptionally talented at cake making, and she graciously offered to provide a cake for our wedding. It turned out absolutely beautifully.

If you don't know someone, I suggest you resist the temptation to spend the money on an expensive cake. You can have a cake without blowing the budget. First of all, stay away from the multi-tiered cakes, which have huge price tags that are largely associated with aesthetics. A slab cake with white frosting that feeds 100 can be great because your guests won't care as long as it tastes good, and you can order a small sized two-tier cake for the cake-cutting ceremony and photos if that's what you want to do. You can also ask the baker if he will decorate a false tier for you. This is just a box that is placed on top of the slab cake, so you can have your pictures taken with it. When you start serving, people will have no idea that there wasn't a real tier on your cake.

You could also go to a grocery store, where the prices are normally very reasonable, and buy a full slab, a half slab and a quarter slab, all with white icing. Stack the slabs of cake, leaving the cardboard in place to steady everything, and use white icing to fill in gaps and pull it together visually. It is then easy enough to decorate the cake using fresh fruit and/or fresh flowers picked on the day of the wedding. This is a simple and inexpensive way to give yourself a tiered cake that you can be proud of.

Using tiers of cupcakes rather than a wedding cake is another trend for budget-conscious couples. You still get the tiered effect—individually decorated cupcakes on tiers of platters looks great—but without the big price tag.

BAR

Everyone loves an open bar—that's what makes receptions so popular. However, it is important to recognize that drinks are a significant portion of your reception expenses. Providing your own alcohol is an important way to save money on your reception. Not only is the cost per drink lower, you take home any partially used bottles, and any unopened wine, liquor or beer that was purchased from a liquor store can be returned for a refund. The cost of using the venue's bar is higher per drink than buying your own and you may pay for alcohol that is not used because you are charged for any bottles that are opened, whether they are finished or not, and you can't take them away. Note that you may find an absolutely fantastic deal on the perfect venue but be required to use their bar rather than provide your own alcohol.

Whether you provide the alcohol yourself or you use the venue for the bar, you will have to decide whether you can afford to have a fully open bar or whether you want to charge for drinks. If you decide that you need to recoup some of the cost of the bar, you have a number of options.

One is to have a donation bar. This is a great concept that we used at our wedding and it worked out great—we recovered a lot of the bar costs. Essentially you have an open bar, but you set up donation boxes. The idea is that your guests will throw in some money and drink roughly that amount's worth. This is nice for your guests because they don't have to worry about specific cash for each drink, they can just make a donation at the beginning of the night. If you have to pay for the venue's bar, this may not cover your bill, but it should certainly help to pay for half of it. If you're using liquor that you've bought yourself, then your bar bill should pretty well be covered using this set up. Depending on the size of the bar at your venue, you will have one or more donation boxes, ideally right where people are going to be ordering their drinks. Also, at the beginning of the reception, have the master of ceremonies (MC) announce something to the effect that the bar is open, but that the bride and groom are accepting donations to help with the cost.

Another way to cut your bar costs is to charge a flat price per drink. The price can still be reasonable for your guests (say $2) and you're guaranteed to recover at least some of your costs. To eliminate the need for your bartenders to handle money and make change, you can have ticket sales. The guests buy their tickets (friends and family are often very helpful in selling tickets) and give a ticket to the bartender for each drink they order.

If you're purchasing your own liquor, you'll need to figure out how much to buy. Go with a four drink multiplier. So, for example, if you have 100 guests, you'll need to buy enough for 400 drinks. A break down of 50% beer, 25% wine and 25% spirits typically works out nicely; however, if you know that your guests are big wine drinkers, you'll want to readjust. Keep in mind that one bottle of beer is one standard drink, a 750 ml bottle of wine is about 5 standard drinks, and a 750 ml bottle of spirits is about 17 drinks. So for our example of 100 guests, you'll need about 200 bottles of beer, 20 bottles of wine and 6 bottles of spirits. You'll also have to buy some pop and juice if the venue doesn't provide it.

You can lower your initial costs for alcohol by using a reputable local make-your-own-wine store. Rather than spending $10 to $12 per bottle of wine from the liquor store (a total of $200 to $250), you can reduce your wine cost in half by making your own wine. If you make your own wine, you will get about 30 bottles for $3.50 to $5.00 per bottle (depending on the style and quality), reducing your cost to between $100 and $150. There are at least a few such companies in almost every community, and you can make very nice wines. You'll need to organize this a few months in advance because the better wines usually improve if they sit for a longer period of time. If it's within a couple of months until your wedding date, you can ask the make-your-own-wine businesses in your area if there are any half batches available for sale that will be ready around the time you need them.

If you really want to be frugal, you can also brew your own beer at a similar establishment. The cost of brew-your-own beer is roughly

$50 for a batch of 50 bottles, or $1 per beer. This could drop your beer cost to about $200 from $300 to $400.

Chapter 9: The Entertainment

Music

The most obvious way to have entertainment at your wedding reception is to have a DJ. They're cost effective because you get a lot of entertainment value for the money, and music really adds to the atmosphere. A good DJ will get your guests dancing and having fun, and many DJ's will act as the MC, making announcements and introducing speeches.

Though it is generally easy to find a DJ, they do vary in price. You should be able to find a DJ with a good reputation for around $700 for the night. Packages will vary in price depending on what sort of sound system and features you want, such as a light show or karaoke.

Some people choose to have a live band at their wedding. This is a little less practical because a band takes up more space, they generally don't play as wide a variety of music and they tend to cost a lot more.

I've also been to some weddings where there are professional dancers that come out and do a show. This is impressive, and it makes the night very festive; however, it doesn't involve the guests and it's just for show. There's nothing that makes your guests have more fun than hitting the dance floor to some solid beats.

Favors

Wedding favors are often given to the guests at the end of the night or are placed on the dinner tables. They are typically a token gift to thank your guests and help them remember your special night. The favor can be anything from a CD of the music being played that night to a small picture or a shot glass. Your guests will generally not remember the favour or the food (as long as it's not bad) or the entertainment. They will remember having a good time at your wedding because of the atmosphere. The more conducive your celebration is to socializing, dancing, eating and drinking, the more memorable it will likely be. Rather than spending money on a favor for each guest to take home, here's a simple idea that will benefit you and your guests.

At the wedding reception have a friend or relative take a picture of every guest (with their significant other as appropriate). Have each guest fill out a card with a personalized message to you and your spouse. At the end of the wedding, rather than having a guest book, you'll have each guest's picture with a personal note. You can then create a photo album with the pictures alongside the notes. When you send out your thank you notes, you can include a copy of the photo, which your guests are much more likely to keep than some trinket. Whenever they see the photo, they'll be reminded of your wedding and what a great time it was.

AFTER THE
WEDDING

"Success in marriage is much more than finding the right person; it is a matter of being the right person."

— ANONYMOUS

HONEYMOON

The honeymoon. Isn't this what all couples are waiting for? You take off to the sunny south to enjoy time together after the hustle and bustle of the wedding and all the stress leading up to it. This book isn't intended to be a travel-planning guide; however, since you've saved so much on your wedding up to this point, I want you to save money on your honeymoon as well.

Traditionally, couples go on their honeymoon immediately or very shortly after their wedding day. Tory and I left for our honeymoon just a few days after the wedding. Depending on the time of year, however, you may not find deals on travel, so think about deferring your honeymoon. On the internet you'll find that lot of travel sites offer special packages and discounts for honeymooners. Many of them will stipulate that you only need to take advantage of the honeymoon deal within six months of your wedding, so this gives you some flexibility and you may be more successfull in finding low cost flights to your destination of choice.

Depending on the time of year, maybe look at going somewhere less traditional for the season. Europe is very busy in the summer and can be very expensive; on the other hand, the Caribbean is very expensive during the winter months. So, if you're doing a fall or winter wedding, maybe look at going to Europe rather than the Caribbean or Mexico. If you're getting married in the summer, you can find some great deals to South America, Mexico and the Caribbean.

YOUR NEW LIFE TOGETHER

Now that the wedding is over, the fun is just about to begin. I look at my grandparents: they've been married for over 60 years and are still as happy as when they were just starting out. It goes to show that great marriages are possible. It's been said that money is the biggest issue that couples argue about. So, why not start out on the right foot. Don't take on tens of thousands of dollars in debt for your wedding day. By using the ideas in this book, you'll be able to begin your married life with a fantastic, memorable wedding day like the one you always envisioned and be able to afford other things you want. Who knows, maybe a down payment on a house!

Extras

Your $7500 Dream Wedding: Budget Breakdown

Preparation

Invitations	$	200.00
Dress	$	500.00
Photographer	$	800.00
Attire	$	150.00

Ceremony

Location	$	250.00
Flowers	$	600.00
Music	$	150.00
Officiant	$	150.00
Transportation (Car or Limo)	$	500.00

Reception

Venue	$	500.00
Catering	$	2,400.00
Cake	$	150.00
Bar	$	850.00
Bar Receipts*	$	-600.00
Decoration	$	300.00
Entertainment	$	600.00
Total:	**$**	**7,500.00**

Bar receipts assumes 100 guests and a $2 per drink charge to your guests, or roughly what you'd receive with a donation bar.

List of Resources

LightInTheBox.com
A great resource for wedding attire including jewelry and clothing

www.lightinthebox.com

American Floral Distributors
You can order discounted flowers to anywhere in the USA, and Canada. Also has free video lessons on various topics such as arranging and making bouquets.

weddingflowersofamerica.com

2G Roses
An online florist that offers discounted flowers. Great way to save money if you can do your own arrangements. Currently only ships within USA.

www.freshroses.com